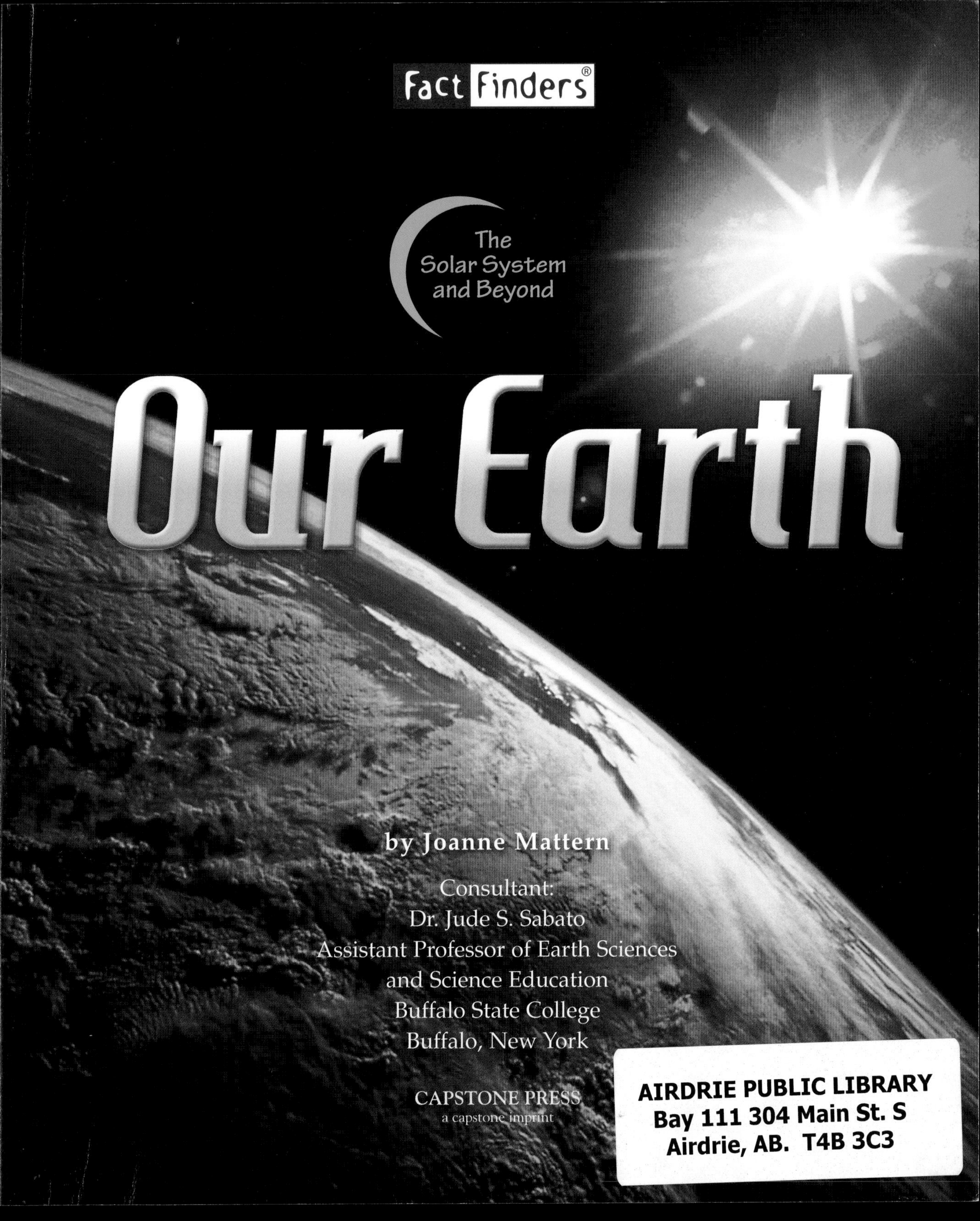

Fact Finders®

The
Solar System
and Beyond

Our Earth

by Joanne Mattern

Consultant:
Dr. Jude S. Sabato
Assistant Professor of Earth Sciences
and Science Education
Buffalo State College
Buffalo, New York

CAPSTONE PRESS
a capstone imprint

Fact Finders are published by Capstone Press,
151 Good Counsel Drive, P.O. Box 669, Mankato, Minnesota 56002.
www.capstonepub.com

Books published by Capstone Press are manufactured with paper
containing at least 10 percent post-consumer waste.

Library of Congress Cataloging-in-Publication Data
Mattern, Joanne, 1963–
Our earth / by Joanne Mattern.
p. cm.—(Fact finders. the solar system and beyond)
Includes bibliographical references and index.
Summary: "Describes planet Earth, including its place in space, earth forms, and
weather"—Provided by publisher.
ISBN 978-1-4296-5395-4 (library binding)
ISBN 978-1-4296-6240-6 (paperback)
1. Earth—Juvenile literature. I. Title. II. Series.
QB631.4.M374 2011
525—dc22   2010026026

Editorial Credits
Jennifer Besel, editor; Heidi Thompson, designer; Laura Manthe, production specialist

Photo Credits
Alamy: David Fleetham, 18, David R. Frazier Photolibrary, Inc., 21, Profimedia International s.r.o.,
11, Universal Images Group Limited, 15; Capstone Press, 9; DigitalVision, 5; iStockphoto: magaliB,
27; NASA, 13; Photodisc, cover, 1, 3, 29; Shutterstock: Andrea Danti, 23, dirkr, 19, George Burba, 20,
Matamu, 7, Pichugin Dmitry, 17, Ralph Loesche, 20

Artistic Effects
iStockphoto: appleuzr, Dar Yang Yan, Nickilford

Printed in the United States of America in Stevens Point, Wisconsin.
072011   006285R

Table of Contents

Chapter 1

Perfect Planet

We all call Earth home. Of all the planets and other bodies in the solar system, Earth is the only place that supports life. That makes our planet one of a kind!

Earth's many features work together to make life possible. Our planet has many different **ecosystems** that are home to a huge variety of plants and animals. These ecosystems are located on landforms such as high mountains and deep caves. Each ecosystem has exactly the right conditions for the living things found there.

Earth is also filled with other special features. Our planet has weather that changes all the time. Plants make the oxygen that all living things need for survival. And the never-ending water cycle keeps life going.

ecosystem: a group of animals and plants that work together with their surroundings

Earth is just one part of our solar system. But it is a spectacular planet in the universe. In space, our home planet spins around and around. While on Earth, life goes on above and below the surface.

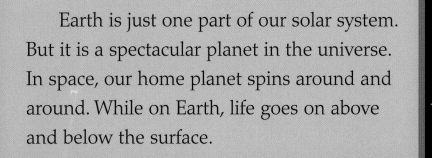

Formed at Just the Right Distance

About 5 billion years ago, a rotating cloud of gas and dust began to collapse in space. Most of the gas and dust fell to the center of the cloud and got very hot. When the gas and dust began to burn, our Sun was born.

Some gas and dust didn't land on the forming Sun. It fell into a disk surrounding the star. Over time, the dust began to clump together, forming bigger and bigger boulders. Eventually, eight planets formed. Earth was one of those planets.

The Sun's **gravity** keeps the planets in place. Earth is known as one of the inner planets because it's fairly close to the Sun. In fact, it's only about 93 million miles (150 million kilometers) away from the fiery star. That might seem like a long distance. But it's actually pretty close in space terms. And it turns out that this distance creates perfect conditions for a planet full of life.

gravity: a force that pulls objects together

If Earth were closer or farther away from the Sun, nothing could live here. Compare Earth's temperature to the temperatures on other planets. Earth's average temperature is 59 degrees Fahrenheit (15 degrees Celsius). But the average temperature on Venus is a toasty 864°F (462°C). If that's too hot, try Neptune, where the average temperature is -353°F (-214°C).

FACT: Dwarf planets, asteroids, and comets are leftovers from when the planets formed. These pieces never made it into a planet.

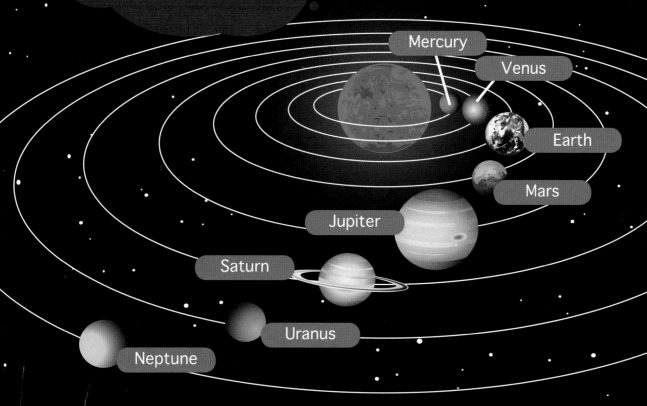

Mercury

Venus

Earth

Mars

Jupiter

Saturn

Uranus

Neptune

Moving Around

The Earth has been spinning since it was born. Our planet moves around the Sun, pulled by the star's gravity. It takes about 365 days, or one year, for Earth to **orbit** the Sun once.

This orbit plays a part in Earth's seasons. Earth's tilt also plays a role. The Earth is tipped 23½ degrees on its **axis**. Scientists think that long ago something hit Earth and pushed it over. So now, as the planet orbits the Sun, the part of Earth tilted toward the heat experiences summer. The half tipped away has winter.

The Earth doesn't just orbit the Sun. It also spins on its axis. As the Earth spins, one side of the planet faces the Sun and has daylight. The other side faces away from the Sun and has night. One rotation of the Earth takes 24 hours, or one full day.

FACT: Earth travels 584 million miles (940 million km) around the Sun at a speed of 18.6 miles (30 km) per second.

orbit: the path an object follows as it goes around a star

axis: an imaginary line that runs through the middle of the planet

Sun

Moon

Earth

axis

Moon's path around Earth

Earth's path around the Sun

Space Neighbor

At night it's easiest to see Earth's closest neighbor. The Moon is a dry, lifeless rock about 238,855 miles (384,400 km) away. Earth's gravity keeps the Moon close by. But the Moon also affects Earth. The Moon's gravity pulls on Earth's oceans and lakes, causing **tides**.

tide: the constant change in sea level

9

Chapter 2

Layers of Earth

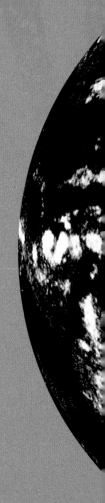

Like other planets, Earth is round. At the equator, Earth is 7,926 miles (12,756 km) around. It might sound like Earth's a huge planet. But it isn't compared it to the other planets in the solar system. Earth is just the fifth largest in size. Jupiter, the largest planet, is about 11 times bigger than Earth. Our planet is tiny compared to the Sun. More than 1 million Earths could fit inside the Sun.

Center of the World

So what exactly is this round, smallish planet made of? Earth is made of three layers. Earth's center is called the core. The core is made of iron and nickel. The outer part of the core is a liquid called magma, while the inner part is a solid iron ball. Both parts of the core are extremely hot. In fact, the core is the hottest place on Earth. Scientists estimate the temperature of the inner core at more than 9,000°F (5,000°C).

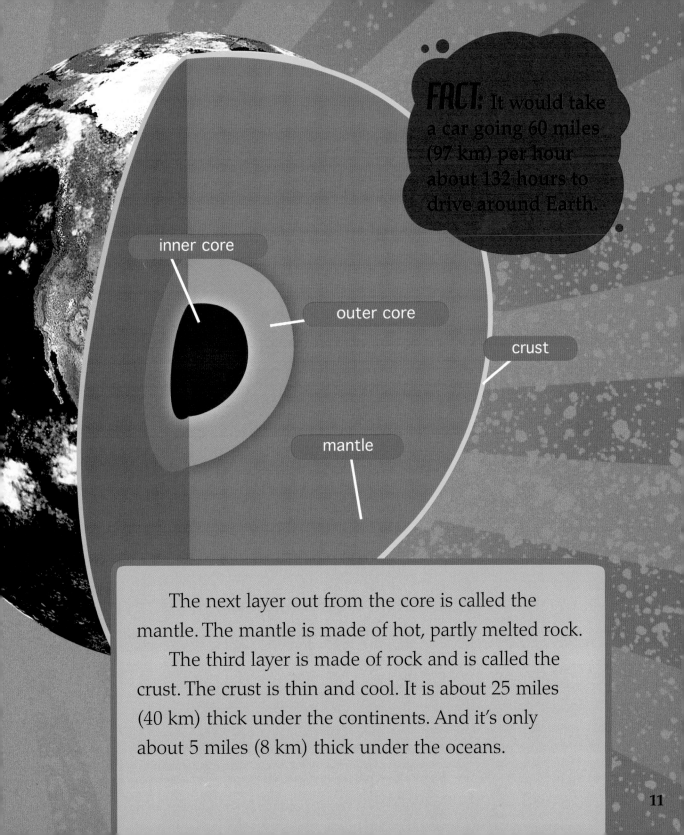

inner core

outer core

crust

mantle

The next layer out from the core is called the mantle. The mantle is made of hot, partly melted rock.
The third layer is made of rock and is called the crust. The crust is thin and cool. It is about 25 miles (40 km) thick under the continents. And it's only about 5 miles (8 km) thick under the oceans.

On the Surface

Above the Earth's crust is the surface. If you look at a photo of Earth taken from space, you'll see that about 71 percent of the planet is blue. All that blue is water. Earth is the only planet that is covered with liquid water.

Most of Earth's water is found in the oceans. Earth has five oceans. The largest is the Pacific Ocean. The other four oceans are the Atlantic, the Indian, the Arctic, and the Southern, or Antarctic. Ocean water is always salty. The salt comes from minerals in Earth's crust that are washed into the oceans by moving water. About 97 percent of Earth's water is salt water.

Earth's other three percent of water is freshwater. Freshwater flows in our planet's lakes and rivers. There's also a lot of freshwater in underground springs. But 68 percent of Earth's freshwater is frozen in ice caps around the North and South Poles.

On Land

The remaining 29 percent of Earth's surface is made up of landmasses called continents. Earth's crust is made of gigantic plates. These plates move and shift. Millions of years ago, plate movement shifted land into seven continents—Asia, Africa, Europe, North America, South America, Australia, and Antarctica. Asia is the largest continent, while Australia is the smallest.

13

In the Air

Above the surface, an atmosphere of gases surrounds Earth. Earth's atmosphere is made up of 78 percent nitrogen, 21 percent oxygen, and 1 percent argon. These gases keep Earth's surface from getting too hot or too cold. The atmosphere also controls weather and **climate** patterns.

Earth's atmosphere is made of five layers. The troposphere is closest to Earth. You walk around in the troposphere every day. This layer is made mostly of two gases—nitrogen and oxygen. The air we breathe comes from the troposphere.

FACT: From the surface, Earth's atmosphere reaches out more than 348 miles (560 km).

The next layer is the stratosphere. If you've ever flown in an airplane, you have traveled into the stratosphere. This part of the atmosphere is home to a layer of gases called the ozone layer. The ozone layer blocks **ultraviolet light** from the Sun. Without this layer, ultraviolet rays would kill plants, animals, and people.

The top three layers of the atmosphere are called the mesosphere, the thermosphere, and the exosphere. Astronauts blast through these layers to go into space.

climate: the usual weather in a place

ultraviolet light: an invisible part of sunlight

Atmosphere

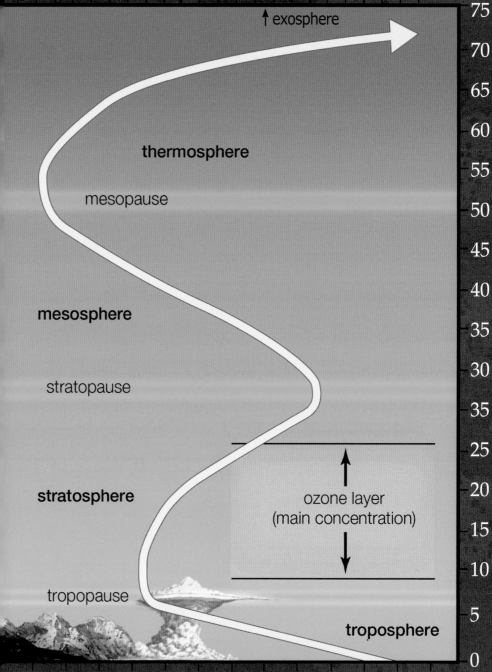

temperature (ºF) (yellow line)

140 -120 -100 -80 -60 -40 -20   0   20   40   60   80

75

↑ exosphere

70

65

60

thermosphere

55

mesopause

50

45

40

mesosphere

35

30

stratopause

35

25

stratosphere

20

ozone layer
(main concentration)

15

10

tropopause

5

troposphere

0

0 -90 -80 -70 -60 -50 -40 -30 -20 -10   0   10   20   30

temperature (ºC) (yellow line)

altitude (miles)

Exploring the Surface

The Earth's surface is a bumpy, lumpy canvas of many different landforms. From mountain peaks to flat prairies, there is a huge variety of natural features on this planet.

The highest places on Earth are mountains. The plates in Earth's crust created these landforms. Mountains form when the plates rub against each other, pushing rock upward. The tallest mountain on Earth is Mount Everest. It stands 29,035 feet (8,850 m) tall. But the plates are still pushing, so the mountain is still growing!

Other places on Earth are flat. Plains are large, flat areas of land. Plains are found on every continent except Antarctica. Most plains are covered with grass and have few tall trees.

Water has helped create many of our planet's landforms. Over thousands of years, water has worn away rock, creating canyons, caves, and valleys. Lakes and rivers are also important landforms. They contain some of the freshwater found on Earth.

The World's Biomes

Earth is home to many different **biomes**. Each biome has its own climate and unique animals and plants that live there. In oceans, deserts, forests, grasslands, and tundras, Earth is full of life.

Earth's largest biome is the ocean. The five oceans make up this huge ecosystem. Thousands of different plants and animals have **adapted** to life in the cold, salty sea. Single-celled plants float in the waves. Earth's biggest animals, blue whales, swim through ocean waters.

biome: a place with a particular climate and certain animals and plants

adapt: to change in order to survive

Deserts are another of Earth's amazing biomes. Deserts receive less than 10 inches (25 cm) of precipitation each year. Desert plants and animals have adapted to a world without water. Cactuses store what little moisture they get in their thick stems. Animals such as coyotes, bats, and elf owls hunt during cool nights and sleep during hot, dry days.

Many plants and animals live in the steamy climate of a tropical rain forest. This biome gets 60 to 400 inches (152 to 1,016 cm) of rain every year. Giant trees tower overhead. Colorful parrots squawk in the branches.

The tundra is the opposite of the rain forest in many ways. The tundra is extremely cold and gets little precipitation. But plants and animals have adapted to this biome. Shrubs and grasses thrive in the short growing seasons. Animals such as arctic foxes and polar bears call the tundra home.

Another biome is the grassland. A grassland is covered with—you guessed it—grass! There are few trees in a grassland, but there is lots of ground cover. Animals such as prairie dogs and bison live in the tall grass of the North American grassland. You'll find herds of zebras and gazelles in African grasslands. All that grass gives the animals plenty of food to eat.

Chapter 4

The World at Work

Earth is unique in the solar system because it has oxygen in its atmosphere. Oxygen became a part of Earth's atmosphere millions of years ago. Erupting volcanoes sent steam into the atmosphere. The Sun's ultraviolet light broke the water droplets in steam into oxygen and hydrogen gases. Hydrogen is lighter than oxygen. So the hydrogen floated away from Earth. The heavier oxygen became trapped in Earth's atmosphere.

Later, plants added more oxygen to the atmosphere. And they continue to do that today in a process called photosynthesis.

Photosynthesis

All plants contain chlorophyll. Chlorophyll gives plants their green color. But it does more than that. It also absorbs sunlight.

Photosynthesis

oxygen

sunlight

carbon dioxide

Inside a plant, chlorophyll catches the Sun's energy. At the same time, the plant's roots drink up water, and its leaves absorb carbon dioxide gas. Inside its cells, the plant uses the Sun's energy to break apart water molecules. These molecules mix with carbon dioxide. The mixture forms a sugar the plant uses as food. As it makes food, the plant releases leftover oxygen from the water molecules into the air. People breathe in that oxygen and breathe out carbon dioxide. That action starts the whole cycle over again.

Weather

Weather is an ever-changing event on Earth. Weather forms in the atmosphere, usually in the troposphere. And it affects every part of life on the planet.

Scientists measure air pressure to forecast the weather. Air pressure is the weight of air pressing down on Earth. The pressure isn't the same everywhere. High on mountains, the pressure is not as strong as on the ground below. The pressure changes because as you go higher, there is less air to push down.

Air temperature affects the pressure too. The Sun heats the air. But the Earth has bumps and lumps. So the air doesn't get heated evenly. Some spots are warm while others are cool. And those warm and cold regions have different air pressures. Cold air is **dense**, so it has a high pressure. Warm air is less dense and has a low pressure.

dense: packed or crowded with more air molecules

In areas of warm, low pressure, the air rises. As it rises, cool air with high pressure moves in to take its place. This movement of air is called wind. As the wind blows, more air rises. The upward movement causes clouds and precipitation to form.

FACT: Every planet except Mercury has an atmosphere that supports weather systems.

orming eather

high pressure

low pressure

Earth

The Water Cycle

Life on Earth could not exist without the water cycle. The water cycle provides freshwater for all living things.

The ocean is a good place to start our tour of Earth's water cycle. Heated by the Sun, ocean water turns into a gas called water vapor. High in the sky, the vapor cools and turns back into droplets of liquid water. These droplets form clouds. When the droplets become big and heavy enough, they fall to the Earth as rain or snow. The rain and snow fill streams and rivers. Rivers eventually flow back into the oceans, starting the water cycle over.

FACT: The water cycle is Earth's way of recycling water. We use the same water that was here when the dinosaurs lived.

1. The Sun's heat turns the water into water vapor.

2. The vapor cools and forms clouds.

3. The water falls back to Earth as rain or snow.

4. The water eventually flows back to the ocean.

Earth's Water Cycle

Chapter 5

No Place Like Home

An old saying states "there's no place like home." For the more than 6 billion people who live here, there is definitely no place like Earth! But as you can imagine, all these people have had a big effect on planet Earth. Like animals and plants, people have adapted their ways of life to survive. At the same time, they have changed Earth. People have cut down forests, drained wetlands, and flooded canyons in order to build homes, businesses, and roads. Chemicals from cars and factories have poisoned the atmosphere, changing Earth's climate.

All that sounds like very bad news, and it is. But there is good news about Earth's future too. People are beginning to realize how much we have damaged Earth. Many people are taking steps to stop the destruction. And so can you. Recycling bottles and using less water are small actions. But those actions can have a big impact on the future of Earth.

Earth is an incredible planet floating around space. Plants push oxygen into the air for people and animals to breathe. Biomes full of beautiful animals cover the land. Water falls from the sky, keeping all living things healthy. From the highest mountains to the deepest oceans, Earth is home to millions of life-forms. And if we all work together, it will be our home for billions of years to come.

Glossary

adapt (uh-DAPT)—to change in order to survive; a change in an animal or plant is called an adaptation

axis (AK-sis)—an imaginary line that runs through the middle of a dwarf planet, moon, or planet; a dwarf planet, moon, or planet spins on its axis

biome (BUY-ome)—an area with a particular type of climate and certain plants and animals that live there

climate (KLY-muht)—the usual weather in a place

dense (DENSS)—thick or crowded

ecosystem (EE-koh-sis-tuhm)—a group of animals and plants that work together with their surroundings

gravity (GRAV-uh-tee)—a force that pulls objects together; gravity increases as the mass of objects increases or as objects get closer

orbit (OR-bit)—the path an object follows as it goes around a dwarf planet, planet, or star

tide (TIDE)—the constant change in sea level that is caused by the pull of the Moon on Earth

ultraviolet light (uhl-truh-VYE-uh-lit LITE)—light from the Sun that people cannot see

Read More

Bow, James. *Earth Mysteries Revealed*. Mysteries Revealed. New York: Crabtree, 2010.

Carson, Mary Kay. *Far-Out Guide to Earth*. Far-Out Guide to the Solar System. Berkeley Heights, N.J.: Enslow Elementary, 2011.

Latham, Donna. *Earth's Biomes*. Life Science. Chicago: Raintree, 2009.

Van Gorp, Lynn. *Landforms*. Mission: Science. Minneapolis: Compass Point Books, 2010.

Internet Sites

FactHound offers a safe, fun way to find Internet sites related to this book. All of the sites on FactHound have been researched by our staff.

Here's all you do:

Visit *www.facthound.com*

Type in this code: 9781429653954

Check out projects, games and lots more at
www.capstonekids.com

Index